7 LESSONS AT 70

Notes from the Front Line

BY SUSAN SOKOL BLOSSER

ILLUSTRATIONS BY JACK OHMAN

"But age became him as it did the oaks and the cedars."
— THOMAS BURNETT SWANN, DAY OF THE MINOTAUR

7 Lessons at 70: Notes From the Front Line

Copyright 2019 by Susan Sokol Blosser

ISBN: 9781091091252

All rights reserved. No part of this book may be reproduced or transmitted in any form or by any means, electronic or mechanical, including photocopying or by any information storage and retrieval system, without written permission from the author, except for the inclusion of brief quotations in a review.

All inquiries should be addressed to:

Susan Sokol Blosser
PO Box 399
Dundee, OR 97115

DEDICATION

To the memory of my mother, Phyllis Sokol, who lived to her 102nd year and showed me that growing old can be beautiful.

NOTE TO READERS

This book developed from a talk I gave in December 2018 at the AARP Portland (Oregon) Vital Aging Conference. I wasn't sure I had anything new to say and was surprised at my reception. My comments were so well received, I was urged to expand my talk into something people could keep to read and reread. It was clear that my message resonated with a generation seeking relevance for this stage of their lives.

Perhaps you have climbed the career ladder and are wondering what comes next. Then this book is for you. Or if you have parents who are facing retirement and questioning what life holds next for them, this book is for them.

Jack Ohman (Editorial Cartoonist at the *Sacramento Bee*) and Bryan Potter (Bryan Potter Design), whose illustrations and design talents shine in my earlier book, *Gracious & Ruthless: Surprising Strategies for Business Success*, came together again to bring this one to life. Jack's drawings not only captured my thoughts, but lightened an often somber subject. And Bryan gave my book a professional and appealing look.

I am grateful for the time, thought, and suggestions that several close friends contributed while I was working on this manuscript. Thank you to Catherine Blosser, Susan Barnes-Whyte, Lan Carpenter, and Lauren McCall. They saw the manuscript through multiple drafts and the result is richer for their comments. My husband, Russ Rosner, performed valuable editing, and nurtured me during the writing process.

Heartfelt thanks to all.

Susan Sokol Blosser
Dayton, Oregon, 2019

CONTENTS

Chapter 1	Aging is Our Frontier	1
Chapter 2	The Three Challenges of Aging	7
	Managing Loss	
	Recapturing Joy	
	Generativity	
Chapter 3	Facing the Challenges of Aging: Elder or Old Fart?	15
Chapter 4	7 Lessons at 70	20
	1. Embrace Your Age	
	2. Past, Present, Future	
	3. Honor Your Inner Self	
	4. Mind, Body, Spirit	
	5. Be of Use	
	6. Be Grateful	
	7. Mentor	
Chapter 5	Final Thoughts	40

Chapter 1

Aging is Our Frontier

"It's not how old you are, but how you are old."
— Marie Dressler

Growing old is not a choice. If you are alive, it's inevitable. What choice you have lies in how you respond. But while past generations had norms and customs to follow, my generation of Baby Boomers has found the traditions of retirement and aging woefully irrelevant. We may be "old" but we are more ready for adventure than our parents' generation. We don't want to be put out to pasture, like an old race horse which performed well in its prime but has nothing left to give. Aging has become the new frontier for my generation. What are the options for us, growing old in the 21st century?

Perhaps your first thoughts when you see the word "frontier" are of places and things. Like the Wild West, or Alaska, or Space. But we are dealing with a different kind of frontier—one we face inside us. And Baby Boomers are confronting a big one—AGING. It's a frontier because none of us have been there before, the old customs don't apply, and we have to learn how to cope. We need to do this for ourselves, but we are also setting a path for future generations to follow.

Our job is to redefine this time in our lives, to set new norms and customs that recognize our priorities. We're up to the task. This is not the first boundary line our generation has crossed. Our first frontier was gender roles. We met it head on and fundamentally created a new playing field for how men and women relate to each other.

Women (and some men) of my generation not only challenged conventional male-female relationships, we reshaped them as we went along. Born in the 1940s and liberated by the birth control revolution of the late 20th century, we listened to Gloria Steinem, cheered for Billie Jean King, and fought for equal rights for women in every arena, from public school and college athletics to workplace equality. We started with the Victorian stance of our mothers, then realized that wasn't going to work for us. We got active in the last third of the 20th century when we came of age, courted, married, and raised families.

At that time, a wife took her husband's surname—it was actually illegal to do otherwise—and women were always referred to by their married title, like Mrs. John Doe. Even the minutes from women's organizations referred to their members by their husbands' name. Reading them, you would have no idea what their first names were, even though the organization was all women. This was a remnant of the days when women were the property of their fathers, and then of their husbands. This convention lingered long after property laws were eliminated, an example of continuing customs that are recognized today as unconscious bias. I'm not ascribing blame. My friends and I looked forward to taking our husbands' names. And by accepting the convention, we women were complicit in the denial of our individuality.

My mother, who came of age in the 1920s, participated in the first feminist push of the century. This is when women got the vote, cut their hair, shed their girdles, wore short skirts, and danced the Charleston. Photos of my mother during that period show her with marcelled hair, wearing a short "flapper" dress. But other than the vote, the changes for women were mainly cosmetic. A professional violinist, my mother did what was expected and stopped work when she got married. I never heard her complain about giving up her career, although she once told me she was making more money than her husband when they married.

Then, in the 1960s when the forces of change were in the air, many women decided male dominance amounted to oppression and had to change. We had no blueprint to guide us and had to work out our new view of relationships as we went along, trying to balance career and children, love and independence, heredity and innovation—determined to go where women had not gone before, to create a culture of true equality.

The result was that gender relations got remixed. Men and women today are still realigning the playing field—an ongoing adjustment and not an easy one. Meanwhile we, who started it all, have grown older and find ourselves facing our next frontier—redefining old age to be relevant to us.

My generation has finally entered "la troisième," the last third of life, and the aging process has my full attention. I'm watching myself grow old—a spectator as well as a participant. Still physically fit and mentally active, I had no idea what lay ahead when I officially retired at age 65. I only knew I wasn't going to sit home. I railed against the word "retirement" after reading its synonyms in my thesaurus. The words suggested by the dictionary—relinquishment, resignation, separation, removal, laying down, exiting, retreating, withdrawal, departure, recession, retreat, regression, abdication, severance—were so unappealing, I tried to think of a synonym I could live with, one that fit my sense of identity. Words like graduation, transformation, and reinvention came to mind. None quite fit.

I want to grow old gracefully, but I'm not sure what that means or how to do it. We have broken the mold but have no replacement. Our expectations differ from past generations. As my friends and I seek to be worthy elders, we find ourselves forging a new model of aging. Our success redefining the relationship between men and women gives us courage. We're used to making it up as we go.

The first step has been to acknowledge that the old ways don't apply to us. The conventional retirement dream was that every day would be like a vacation—your time to concentrate on yourself—sit in your rocking chair, in between golf and bridge. For my friends and me, that wasn't enough. Whether we fought or protested, the Vietnam War got us involved, and we have been active in our communities ever since.

Modern medicine has kept us healthier and more mobile so we know redefining retirement will include activity, and ideally, productive activity. But we also know time is relentless. We will continue to age and must be proactive, both physically and emotionally to meet whatever challenges that brings. Physically, it's not about fighting wrinkles and sagging skin—that's a losing battle. We must learn to appreciate what it took to develop those "wisdom lines." Rather, it's keeping our skeletons strong with exercise and strength training.

Experts are quick to list the challenges of aging and how to meet them. Most tell us what to do—how to act to live longer. They are all important. But the three challenges that resonate with me speak to emotional health—critical to the quality of life. They're appropriate at any age, but become especially important the older we become.

Chapter 2

The Three Challenges of Aging

> "Do not regret growing older.
> It is a privilege denied to many."
> — Author Unknown

> "It behooves me to remember as I advance in age that death is an inevitable part of the life cycle rather than a medical failure."
> — Lisa J. Shultz

The first challenge of aging is Managing Loss. Loss comes at us in many forms. We may first feel this as physical loss—the pull of gravity under our eyes, around our mouths, on our limbs; lost waistline, wrinkled skin, painful joints. If you have always been physically beautiful or handsome, this would be especially hard. If you've been active physically, you could find yourself grieving over no longer being able to race up and down stairs, or go through a twelve hour day and still have energy.

Loss of stamina means we can't do the amount of activity we did when younger. Our energy level starts a downward spiral which no amount of healthy eating can erase. Learning to take time to recover after a burst of activity suits our new situation. Short naps become a welcome respite. I know I can't keep up the same pace I used to and have to listen to my body. We can try to stay in shape with exercises and physical activity, even get surgical help, but really, there is no going back. Old age has a beauty of its own which we can, and must, learn to appreciate.

But more important than physical loss, are the emotions we feel around loss. We feel loss emotionally when we retire from a job where we made a critical contribution. We're left without the identity of a title and position. Where once we were important, suddenly we are no longer needed. That is the "put out to pasture" syndrome. I experienced this when I turned control of the business I had worked in all my adult life, over to my children. I found myself mourning, even though stepping back was my choice. I had to learn that my grieving was a natural reaction.

I had orchestrated a transition with a three year plan. It turned out to be the hardest thing I'd ever done. I kept asking myself "Why am I having such a hard time? This was my decision." What bothered me had nothing to do with my children. They were fully competent. The problem was me. I didn't want to go back, I just couldn't go forward. I had no idea it would be so hard to let go. More about this later.

And, of course, as we age we feel the biggest loss as loved ones—friends, family, companion animals—seem to start dying off at an accelerated rate. Grief at losing a loved person or pet is natural, a small consolation for the price you pay for being able to love. You were lucky enough to have a special relationship, and losing that ruptures something inside of you. Rebuilding a broken heart means working through the grief process of shock, suffering, and release.

Trying to repress or deny your grief just impedes the process. Time is your friend as you find and adjust to a new normal. Work through your grief; don't let it define you forever.

In addition to managing your own loss, you will undoubtedly also face the challenge of being there for a friend who is facing loss and grieving. Talking about loss is sobering; we need to recognize and accept it. Dying is part of life; there's no way to sugarcoat it. Grief counselors advise listening, not probing, letting your friend share what they want to share, and being empathetic.

Fortunately, the next two challenges are more upbeat.

"Never cease to stand like curious children before the great mystery into which we were born."
— ALBERT EINSTEIN

"Many people are alive but don't touch the miracle of being alive."
— THICH NHAT HANH

The second challenge of aging has been described as Recapturing Joy. To me this means reconnecting to the wonderment of life one felt as a child—delighting in the beauty of a bud opening into a flower, marveling at the miracle of a tiny seed becoming a plant, feeling pleasure in the soothing sound of a cat purring, stopping to wonder at the otherworldliness of cloud formations—you get the picture. It means intentionally looking for joy in your life, especially in little things.

You may not be used to stopping what you're doing to observe something that gives you a burst of joy. It's time to start. I feel joy every spring walking in our family vineyard, when the swelled buds on the vines suddenly burst one day. The tiny leaves start to unfurl with rosy tipped edges. Miniature clusters appear. I am filled with awe at this annual rebirth. Noticing daffodils lighting up the cloudy winter days gives me the same feeling. But it doesn't have to be Nature that moves you. It could be a certain line of a poem or a musical piece that sparks joy in your heart. Find what gives you that inner light and take time to notice it.

Joy is different from happiness. Happiness is a byproduct. You feel happy when things go your way, when you have the satisfaction of achieving something you wanted. It could be something big, like landing a sought-after contract at work, getting a promotion, being honored in some way. Or something smaller from everyday life, like learning a new piece on the piano, producing a perfect tomato in your garden, or even finishing a difficult jigsaw puzzle. The pride of achievement makes you happy.

Happiness comes from a satisfied ego. You feel it in your head. Joy is different—it is a direct connection to the heart. You feel joy when you connect to the wonder of the universe, something bigger than you. This feeling is always available, if you choose to access it, regardless of your mood. You could be miserable, yet feel joy hearing a robin sing outside your window or seeing a puppy frolic in the grass. Listening to a Beethoven symphony can trigger joy despite being angry or sad. One of the opportunities of aging is having time to appreciate small things that we might have overlooked in the chaos of raising a family and rising in the workplace.

Giving your spirit a small shot of wonderment helps dissipate negative emotions. Once you figure out and connect with what brings you joy, savor it. Go back to it often. Get out of your own misery by taking time to notice one of Nature's miracles.

⚡

> "If there's one thing I've learned in my years on this planet, it's that the happiest and most fulfilled people are those who devoted themselves to something bigger and more profound than merely their own self-interest."
>
> — JOHN GLENN

The third challenge of aging is described as Generativity. This big, awkward word suggests expanding one's world, continuing to grow, and paying forward to the next generation. Think of it as continuing to have a sense of purpose. Many people, as they age and are no longer trying to further their career, limit their involvement with others and the outside world. They close in, taking literally the traditional synonyms of retirement—severance, withdrawal, and retreat—and form a wall around themselves which nothing new penetrates.

But our world doesn't have to shrink with age. Old age does not need to be synonymous with stagnation. As we redefine retirement, we realize that, rather than being put out to pasture, release from an everyday job gives us time to use what we've learned to give our lives new meaning. Maybe you want to learn something new which got put off earlier because there was never enough time. Pursuing one's interests and staying vital is what determines whether we get stuck in the past or embrace the present.

A librarian I know always wanted to paint but had no time to pursue this interest while she was running a college library. When she retired from that job, she took classes, started painting, and eventually sold her work at art showings. She also paid forward her skills by volunteering at a local literacy nonprofit. In choosing these two activities, she satisfied her inner self, her sense of being, as well as her public self, her sense of doing—that's generativity.

> "You are never too old to set another goal or to dream a new dream."
>
> — C.S. Lewis

Chapter 3

Facing the Challenges of Aging: Elder or Old Fart?

"If you are pining for youth I think it produces a stereotypical old man because you only live in memory, you live in a place that doesn't exist. Aging is an extraordinary process where you become the person you always should have been."

— David Bowie

How well will you manage these three challenges? I have a friend who sums up the alternatives with a blunt question: Do you want to be an Elder or an Old Fart? The mind conjures up two distinctly clear images with this question.

To be an Elder with a capital E, the ideal is that your past has weathered you, imparting a compassionate wisdom which you give away as you move forward. An Old Fart would be stuck in the past, complaining a lot, bitterly resenting the present, devoid of joy. You probably know both. But, here's the quandary—nothing prepares us for Elderhood.

Throughout our education and career, all the buzz, all the focus, is on getting ahead and being the best at whatever you choose to do. We spend years accumulating knowledge, friends, influence, material well-being, accomplishment and accolades. Nobody talks about what happens next—in other words, about letting go of what you have acquired. Not physical things, but rather passing on what you have learned to the next generation.

I happened upon the following unattributed quote, which made everything fall into place. "In the end, only three things matter: how much you have loved, how gently you have lived, and how gracefully you have let go." The quote caught my attention because, at the time, I was in the middle of stepping back at work and finding giving up control far more difficult than anticipated. It was then I realized that no one talked about the letting-go phase, which had led me to assume it would take place easily and naturally. To me, this quote about love, grace, and letting go captures the essence of living an honorable life, perhaps the best description of what being an Elder comprises.

Let's take these one at a time.

How much you have loved.

"It annoys me when people say, 'Even if you're old, you can be young at heart!' Hiding inside this well-meaning phrase is a deep cultural assumption that old is bad and young is good. What's wrong with being old at heart, I'd like to know? Wouldn't you like to be loved by people whose hearts have practiced loving for a long time?"

— Susan Moon

If you think of love as a muscle that grows stronger the more it's used, your capacity for love grows the more you love. If the older you are, the more capacity you have for giving love, it follows that an advantage of aging is that we have a lot of love to give. Where will you bestow all that love? Family, community, the earth? The Elder would have a heart full of love to give away. The love muscle of an Old Fart would be flabby from lack of exercise. Which will you be?

How gently you have lived.

"The Earth does not belong to us: we belong to the Earth."

— Marlee Matlin

Gently suggests concern and humility— treading lightly on the earth and holding a sense of one's impermanence and insignificance in the natural world. I like to think the Elder would accept this and the Old Fart would rail against it. "This is my property and I can do whatever I want," is a typical Old Fart position. Understanding that you are only a temporary custodian of your property would be characteristic of an Elder.

As children we believe the world revolves around us. As we grow up, we expand our world to include family and friends, but seldom is there a sense of how fleeting our lives are in the rhythm of the universe. The years of being the center, of believing that our time on earth is all that matters, have to be reversed as we learn to live gently.

The poet William Stafford ended his poem, The Well Rising, with a sentence that encapsulates for me the essence of living gently:

"I place my feet with care in such a world."

How gracefully you have let go.

"Wisdom, compassion, and courage are the three universally recognized moral qualities of men."
— CONFUCIUS

Grace has a spiritual quality which implies humility, gratitude, and equanimity, qualities beyond the conventional definitions of charm, good humor, or competence. Letting go with grace manifests in different ways. Probably the most spiritual element is being able to receive grace, from others and from yourself. How does receiving grace relate to the concept of letting go? The answer is that you have to let go of that little judge that sits on your shoulder and tells you you're not worthy. Most of us have grown up listening to that disapproving voice and struggling to silence it. Old age is the time to squelch it forever. Believe in yourself. Be able to receive. You wouldn't have made it this far if you weren't worthy.

Knowing when to let go emotionally is an important skill at any age. It takes on more significance the older one gets. Each episode of physical letting go requires an emotional readjustment, sometimes a reinvention of who you are, especially if your identity was defined by what you just let go. If you had children, you first experienced letting go when your youngest child started school, and later when you sent that child off to college or the workplace, knowing that this person you devoted your life to raising was growing away from you and might never live at home again.

Stepping back from a long career which shaped your identity requires letting go of that persona. This applies to any matter of work to which you became attached. School teacher, auto mechanic, retail clerk, accountant, ski instructor, state legislator—retiring from whatever you've been doing that was the center of your working day severs the social connections that inevitably form over years of working side by side.

Another emotional aspect is the ability to let go of harmful or angry feelings you may have been harboring for weeks, or even years. Negative feelings fester and gnaw away at us. Anger at parents or a sibling for something they did when you were young, resentment of a co-worker's comments, anger at yourself for not living up to your expectations, are all common examples. Even though we know anger poisons our insides, we cling to it. Letting go of these feelings liberates you. Sometimes, if you can reframe how you think about something that angers or depresses you, it can be the key to releasing the poison inside. For example, if your view of a childhood event could be interpreted differently, from another person's perspective, it could give you insight and change your understanding. I can give a personal example.

For years, I was upset at my mother because I thought she had an image of the daughter she wanted and tried to make me into that image. I wanted her to accept me for who I was, not who she wanted me to be. Then one day, years after she had died, I got to thinking and realized that I had an image of the mother I wanted and she didn't fit that image. In other words, I was doing the same thing to her I accused her of doing to me. This insight humbled me, completely dissipated my anger, and allowed me to think about my mother differently. I suddenly remembered all the wonderful parts of my childhood instead of the strains.

Letting go, not only well, but with grace, will make you a true Elder.

> *"He that cannot forgive others breaks the bridge over which he must pass himself."*
>
> — EDWARD HERBERT

Chapter 4

7 Lessons at 70

"For the unlearned, old age is winter; for the learned, it is the season of the harvest."

— Hasidic saying

This brings me to what I have learned in my quest to be an Elder rather than an Old Fart. Here are my 7 Lessons at 70, told with the three challenges of aging in mind.

Lesson #1: Embrace Your Age

"Getting old is like climbing a mountain; you get a little out of breath, but the view is much better!"

— Ingrid Bergman

"You can't help getting older, but you don't have to get old."

— George Burns

I am facing the inescapable fact that I am now in my 70s and there is no going back. The possibility of infirmity comes closer with each

passing year. When I turned 60, an age that had seemed so far away, I sensed I had entered the realm of old age. But I didn't feel old, and people told me 60 was the new 40. It was about that time that my first grandchild was born, and I couldn't imagine that I was old enough to fall in that group of ancients. My image of grandparents was that they were old and frail. That wasn't me. I found myself wincing when I was referred to as grandma. But I also felt I was entering a new phase, and it was then I started thinking about what this time of life would mean for me.

It took me ten years to accept the aging process. Old age and death once seemed far away. No longer. As friends my age die, I'm more aware than ever of my mortality. The challenge of managing loss has become real.

Individuals to whom I feel close have become more significant. We meet many people over the years and have different friends at different times in our lives. Our best buddies in high school or college may be distant memories in later life. But whatever your age, there are a few you feel close to. You care about them, confide in them, and work at being a good friend. They are your soulmates. Cherish them. Close friends become ever more important the older you are. With what time is left to you, you can choose carefully who you want to spend it with.

Family falls in a different category. Some families are close, others not so much. Yet whether there is acrimony or love, these are the people who share your unique history and memories. I have three brothers who are even older than I. Our time together is shrinking. When they are gone, there will be no one left to call me by my childhood nickname, or who share the same memories of our parents, recollections that become dearer with each passing year. We are very different, and often disagree, but our familial story ties us together.

Lesson #2: Past, Present, Future

"The great thing about getting older is that you don't lose all the other ages you've been."
— Madeleine L'Engle

"The path to wisdom is a lifelong journey."
— Unknown

The entirety of your life lives within you. Your past has shaped you and prepared you for your future. Consider all you've been through. When you reach 70, you have a lot of history. Some of it you might not want to think about—times where you failed in one way or another. You disappointed someone, made an unforgivable mistake, lost a big sale, got dumped by a lover, couldn't stick to a diet—there are so many ways, big and small, to feel like a failure. They're part of you and hopefully your biggest learning experiences.

There are also undoubtedly times you succeeded. Your team won a big game, you landed a difficult sale, received an A+ on a paper or a commendation at work, you were elected to head something you cared about, maybe you even won the lottery. Was your success a humbling or boasting experience? (Think Elder or Old Fart). Learning from failure and coping with success are flip sides of the coin and equally important to learn from. Few things are worse than a sore loser, unless it's an arrogant winner.

Thinking about the past, coming to terms with all you have done in your life, seeing the patterns of success and failure, is an exercise singularly appropriate to old age. Memories can be bittersweet—painful, nostalgic, tender, joyful, sometimes all at once. Invite them in, linger over them. Glean what you can from the failures, then put them away in a box on the history shelf. Bask in the successes, think how you can build on them, and move forward.

Be grateful for all that you learned and proud that you survived. Now you have time to share your wisdom.

> "Wisdom comes from experience, but experience is not enough. Experience anticipated and experience revisited is the true source of wisdom."
>
> — JOHN GRINDER

Lesson # 3: Honor Your Inner Self

"When we get too caught up in the busyness of the world, we lose connection with one another—and ourselves."

— Jack Kornfield

"The essence of bravery is being without self-deception."

— Pema Chödrön

It's humbling to realize, after so many years of acting on "shoulds and oughts" that, when given the freedom, I had to think hard about what I wanted. It sounds absurd, even sad, to think that someone who has lived so many years doesn't know herself. But our lives are full of responsibilities to others and those roles determine what we do to a great extent. Like so many of us, I knew what I needed to do for my children, for my business, for my aging parents, for my spouse and our home, and I did it without stopping to ask myself what I would choose. I now think of this as my outer persona, fueled by obligation. Old age, in giving me permission to make what I previously considered "selfish" decisions, has helped me discover who I am underneath the layers of duty.

Aging has allowed me to be more ruthless about my time. I look differently now at invitations, opportunities, and requests. Whereas the old me would have automatically jumped into action, I now stop myself and take time to think and quiz myself. When offered opportunities which would have been important to accept when I was climbing the career ladder, I ask questions. Do I really want to do

this? Not what I need to do; not what I should do. This is not as easy as it sounds. After years of acting out of obligation, deciding what I really wanted took deliberate effort. Sometimes what I decided, when

I took time to think about it, surprised me. Something I would have previously discarded as not relevant, suddenly interested me. And, because I still have obligations, I may decide to do something, knowing it's not my first choice. I can't ignore my public persona, but I can recognize the inner one and feed it as much as possible.

Have you always dreamed of doing something you considered unattainable—learning calligraphy, riding a horse, being a Master Gardener, whitewater rafting, knitting a sweater, designing clothes? I could go on and on with possibilities. Did the thought of not being good enough hold you back? Here's your chance. Take to heart the Nike slogan —Just Do it! Once you accept that you don't have to be perfect, a world of new experience opens up to you.

A friend mentioned she was taking piano lessons from a wonderful teacher. I asked what made the teacher wonderful. She didn't hesitate. "She's not judgmental and encourages rather than scolds me." I immediately thought back to all the times I was chastised by the piano teachers of my youth for not practicing enough or playing perfectly the assigned piece. I gave up playing, ashamed I would never be a pianist. Hearing my friend, the idea of playing the piano again, with encouragement instead of reproach, now sounded like fun. So, even though I hadn't played the piano for over 50 years, I started piano lessons.

Limbering up stiff fingers, finding the right notes with each hand and then putting it all together—ever so slowly—has been satisfying. I lose track of time as all my attention is needed to work both hands to find the right notes. I will never excel at this, but that's okay. The goal of perfection which fueled my professional life is no longer important. My teacher understands I'm doing this just for me. How wonderful to know I'll never have to perform or participate in a recital.

Lesson #4: Mind, Body, Spirit

> "It is health that is real wealth and not pieces of gold and silver."
>
> — Mahatma Gandhi

Aging places health concerns front and center. Even if you've always enjoyed good health, you can no longer take it for granted. I know from experience that when you don't feel well, nothing else matters. To maintain quality of life as you age, you need to stay healthy, and the older you get, the more work it takes.

The good news is that you probably now have more time to devote to this important part of your life—an advantage of stepping back from full time work. Because good health involves so much discipline, think of this undertaking as an obligation. It's a commitment you make to yourself. No one else can do it for you. Making your health a priority is a gift not only to yourself, but also to your loved ones.

First, consider what to eat. Metabolism slows with age, so it takes less and less food to gain weight. If you love to eat, like I do, this is really bad news. But even my skinny friends accumulate more bulk with each passing year. It seems to start with the torso. We all seem to be squaring off. Forget the fries and chips. Vegetables, fruits, and fish—all the foods health experts recommend for good health, should now form the basis of your meals.

I do my best to follow that regime, although a large slice of carrot cake, with cream cheese frosting and coconut flakes, hovers in the back of my mind, and it's always beckoning. Sugar is as addictive as any drug. The more sweets I eat, the more I want. I try not to give in to the temptation to bake, because I know I can, and may, devour

what I make. Accepting the limitations of diet that aging imposes will always be a challenge.

Our one weapon is exercising, which I know is good on multiple levels. The benefits of exercise more than compensate for the bowl of chips, or the cookie. Exercise has proven to promote brain health, enhance sleep quality, raise energy level, prevent memory loss, and reduce the threat of chronic disease. With so many benefits, why is it so hard to get going? One word: inertia.

Getting up off the comfort of the couch or easy chair to exercise takes motivation and determination, even though we know this is what we have to do to thrive and not simply survive. Tracking your exercise could help motivate you. A simple thing like carrying a Fitbit can give you incentive to exercise more. I consult mine regularly, competing with myself to see how many steps I can take in a day. Making exercise entertaining by using headphones helps if you're exercising alone. Making it a social occasion by going to a gym to work out, especially with a friend, helps too. Committing to a class can also work to get you up and out.

Moving the body is important, but there's more. Tracking steps is not enough. If you don't want your bones to disintegrate as you age, you need strength training. Lifting weights on a regular program is now recommended in all the literature on aging. You can minimize pharmaceuticals, and all their side effects, if you get on a good program to make your musculature strong.

You have the power. The right foods and a good level of cardio and bone strengthening activity will help keep you at your best. You will never have the body of a 20 or even 40 year old, no matter how well you manage aging. Even healthy, fit bodies can't avoid the wear and tear of age. Teeth need attention as gums recede and enamel thins. Eyes develop cataracts. Joints become arthritic. Proper medical care often requires surgery, from which it takes ever longer to recover. Managing physical loss is not easy, but the benefits of being as healthy as possible make the efforts needed worth it.

Okay, we've dealt with your physical self. How about your mental well being? Old age is notorious for depression, but it doesn't have to be—another difference between Elder and Old Fart. My Lessons #5 and #6 speak to what it takes to maintain the fire inside, but I want to suggest an additional practice that you may find beneficial—meditation. There are many ways to have a meditation practice. You could be sitting on a rock next to a pond, doing yoga, kneeling on a small rug in a meditation hall with others, walking on a nature trail, even just sitting in a chair at home. They all have one thing in common—you are taking time out to be within yourself, quieting your mind—concentrating on just being, and connecting to the wonder of the universe. Done for five to fifteen minutes every day, you will find yourself feeling refreshed, renewed, less stressed, and probably more creative.

> "The body benefits from movement, and the mind benefits from stillness."
>
> — SAKYONG MIPHAM

> "Meditation is a silent heart, a peaceful mind which can make life more lovable, more livable."
>
> — ANONYMOUS

Lesson #5: Be of Use

"*Any decision you make is not a decision about what to do. It's a decision about who you are.*"

— NEALE DONALD WALSCH

If you're no longer climbing the career ladder, you might be feeling the challenge of Generativity, of finding a new sense of purpose. Stepping back from full time work puts you in the position of wondering what you will do to supply the challenge and sense of productivity to keep you engaged. Without the pressure of a job, staying productive is entirely in your hands. Leisure time may be a welcome change, but what if you want to use what you've learned to make a difference? You have knowledge and wisdom to share and your challenge now is to find the equilibrium between your inner and outer personas, between being and doing.

When I was working full time, all my focus was on the business. It consumed my emotional as well as actual time. It took me a few years to find my bearings but I know it's possible to find ways to both challenge yourself, feel productive, and still satisfy your inner being. Life becomes more balanced as you gradually learn to integrate your activities and interests to include some you do just for you and some you do to help others.

I have friends whose examples inspire me. One retired from her nursing career and, following a long time interest, started volunteering at a local historical society. She and her husband joined the local archeological society, learned new skills, made new friends, and volunteered on state and federal archeological excavations. She attended an exercise class she liked so much that when the instructor announced she was quitting, my friend convinced the instructor to train her. She took over and kept the class going, which consisted mostly of health conscious elders.

There are so many opportunities to make a difference and follow an interest which you probably never had time to pursue. Some friends have joined the SMART (Start Making A Reader Today) Program and go weekly to read to kids at their local schools. Others work regularly at a local church's soup kitchen, help restore nature trails, give tours at museums, or volunteer at Headstart. Nonprofits everywhere are crying for help, and there's one for virtually every possible interest and skill. Check with your local Chamber of Commerce for a list if you don't know where to start.

If you can't find a nonprofit that speaks to you, and you see a need that's not being met, get a group of friends together and start one. You have to apply to the state and federal governments for nonprofit status, but getting that allows you to take in tax deductible donations. Your life experience is worth sharing. Don't waste it with inaction.

> "I believe the second half of one's life is meant to be better than the first half. The first half is finding out how you do it. And the second half is enjoying it."
>
> — Frances Lear

Lesson #6: Be Grateful

> "When I started counting my blessings, my whole life turned around."
>
> — Willie Nelson

Whatever pathways your life has taken, you will undoubtedly have endured pain, disappointment, and loss. No one escapes life's blows. Yet there will always be something to be grateful for. Sometimes, being grateful is what happens when you reframe how you look at something. Your kids are so busy with their jobs and families you never see them? Be grateful they have a full life. The dog you've loved for ten years just died? Be grateful you had the experience of a wonderful companion.

This is the bittersweet part of living. "The sorrows that had come to us with the death of loved ones were in direct proportion to the joy each, in life, had brought...." wrote Hannah G. Solomon, founder of the National Congress of Jewish Women, in her autobiography, Fabric of My Life. Being thankful is not simply a Pollyanna approach to life. It's the way to survive hardship and loss. "Gratitude is not a virtue but a survival skill, and our capacity for it grows with our suffering," notes clinical psychologist Mary Pipher.

We live in such a fast-paced world, it's easy to forget being grateful when things go wrong and anxiety takes over. I know from experience that wallowing in self pity depresses me, severely hindering my quality of life. When I feel down, gratitude helps me dig out of the hole I worked myself into. It changes my perspective and I feel better. If you make being grateful, for things large and small, a daily habit, you'll be surprised how much brighter the world will look.

If you're not sure how to begin, here's a suggestion. Designate a special receptacle as your Gratitude Jar. It could be a simple mason jar or a decorated container. Every day, starting with "I'm grateful...." handwrite your thought on a slip of paper and put it in the jar. You could have one Gratitude Jar for each family member or one to which everyone in the household contributes. Then, set a time to read the slips out loud to each other. Make it a regular ritual and you'll find it a beautiful and moving experience. Multiple studies have shown that practicing gratitude enhances positive emotions and empathy. In addition, you'll sleep better, be more compassionate towards yourself and others, and increase your resilience and mental strength.

> "The turning point in the process of growing up is when you discover the core of strength within you that survives all hurt."
>
> — MAX LERNER

Lesson #7: Mentor

> "As you grow older, you will discover that you have two hands, one for helping yourself, the other for helping others."
>
> — Audrey Hepburn

> "A mentor is someone who allows you to see the hope inside yourself."
>
> — Oprah Winfrey

Mentoring suddenly seems everywhere in the news. Many schools and businesses have formal mentoring programs and there seem to be varying definitions. Let me describe what I mean by the term. I'm not interested in a formal structure with appointments and reports. A mentor doesn't have to be a PhD or a therapist. With your life experience, you can be a mentor. You may feel you have nothing to offer, but that's not true. You don't have to be special, you just have to be there and care. This is paying forward what you learned over the course of your career and the people who were there for you.

Mentoring can be the informality of just being interested, listening without judging, asking questions, and offering relevance from your experience. I try to do this with the women I work with. If I can pass along what I have learned, especially to younger women making their way in the business world, I am happy.

There were no mentors when my husband and I started a vineyard and winery in Oregon in the 1970s. We were at the cutting edge of developing a new industry in the state. There was no one experienced

enough to train or lead us. Oregon's wine industry was too new and our situation was different enough from established wine regions that we had to forge our own path. We survived because the few of us who were there helped each other. We learned to collaborate and share our knowledge. We weren't mentors; we were peers.

I longed for a mentor. With no training in farming or business, I had to learn to manage through a combination of research, observation, and trial and error. There were no women I knew who were doing what I was doing. It was a solo quest in a new industry and I was lonely. Not until I got out in the market to sell my wine did I meet women who were trained in sales, who had the experience I lacked. I finally found a small coterie of experienced women who took me under their wing and shared their wisdom with me. Their guidance helped me succeed. They made me understand the profound difference mentoring offers.

Now, without the pressures of developing and running a business, and with the perspective of age, mentoring has taken on increased meaning as an aspect of letting go, in the sense of passing along what I have learned, after a life of accumulation.

> "We're here for a reason. I believe a bit of the reason is to throw little torches out to lead people through the dark."
>
> — WHOOPI GOLDBERG

Chapter 5

Final Thoughts

"It's like you trade the virility of the body for the agility of the spirit."

— Elizabeth Lesser

What an interesting time of life. With no desire to go backwards, I'm curious what the future holds. In my mind, aging falls in the category of experiences one has to live through to understand—experiences that can be appreciated but not fully grasped by study, or even observation (giving birth is another one). My kids listen and nod when I try to explain the physical and mental changes I've experienced, but I know old age to them seems far away and irrelevant. It certainly did to me as I watched my parents age. I never thought it would happen to me. Remember how inviolate we felt in our youth?

Aging has been full of surprises. While the physical may be in decline, the mental and emotional have grown stronger. I'm amazed to find more joy in my life than ever. Power and success—happiness as our world defines it—can be won by fighting hard enough. It's the triumph of one's outer self. But joy, peace, and love come from inside. I had to live for many years to claim that.

I know now that our lives bear an up and down rhythm of good and difficult times. Neither last. We yearn for the security of permanence, but the stability we seek leads to stagnation, the opposite of vitality. As a child I envisioned being "grownup" as a permanent state one achieved at a certain age, somewhere really old, like thirty. Adults reinforced this idea by always asking: "What do you want to be when you grow up?" I learned to have an answer ready, although I've never been any of the professions I imagined between ages five and twenty—jockey, ballerina, United Nations translator, attorney, historian. Instead I've done things I'd never imagined—farmer, business owner, author, nonprofit leader. I have learned that stability is ephemeral, a goal not only impossible but crippling were it to be achieved.

Life is truly a journey into uncharted territory. I look forward to what happens next. I will remind myself to delight in the unexpected and embrace it with wonder. The three challenges of aging—managing loss, recapturing joy, and generativity—are much on my mind as I face the future. Here are two quotes which I hope will inspire you as they do me.

> "Anyone who keeps the ability to see beauty never grows old."
> — Franz Kafka

> "Life isn't about finding yourself. Life is about creating yourself."
> — George Bernard Shaw.

About the Author

Wine industry pioneer, community leader, environmental advocate, and author, Susan Sokol Blosser is a contemporary Oregon icon. When women were rarely decision makers in business or agriculture, Susan distinguished herself in both. Under her presidency, Sokol Blosser Winery became known as one of the most innovative and respected Oregon wineries.

Susan holds a B.A. from Stanford University, an M.A.T. from Reed College, and an Honorary Doctorate of Public Service from the University of Portland, citing her entrepreneurship within the context of environmental and social responsibility. She holds a Lifetime Achievement Award from the Oregon Wine Board and was the first non-Californian woman inducted into the national Women for WineSense Hall of Fame.

She and her husband, Russ Rosner, Sokol Blosser's Winemaker Emeritus, live at the vineyard with 2 cats, 2 Tibetan Terriers, 13 chickens, and 12 koi.

About the Illustrator

Jack Ohman has been the Editorial Cartoonist at the Sacramento Bee since 2013. He won the 2016 Pulitzer Prize for editorial cartooning, and was a finalist for the Pulitzer in 2012. His work is syndicated by The Washington Post Writers Group. Among other national prizes won was the Robert F. Kennedy Journalism Award. He also won Den Genius in 1970 for Cub Scout Pack 1131.

He is married to Amanda V. Ohman, has three grown children all of whom are polite and employed, and has drawn over 10,000 editorial cartoons. He refuses to age, he says.

Made in the USA
Middletown, DE
14 June 2022